GUIDELINES
for Leading Your Congregation

SMALL MEMBERSHIP CHURCH

Creating effective ministries in your church

Written by Julia Kuhn Wallace
General Board of Discipleship

SMALL MEMBERSHIP CHURCH

Copyright © 2000 by Cokesbury

All rights reserved.

United Methodist churches and other official United Methodist bodies may reproduce up to 500 words from this publication, provided the following notice appears with the excerpted material: From *Small Membership Church: 2001–2004*. Copyright © 2000 by Cokesbury. Used by permission.

Requests for quotations exceeding 500 words should be addressed to Permissions Office, Abingdon Press, P.O. Box 801, 201 Eighth Avenue South, Nashville, TN 37202-0801.

This book is printed on elemental-chlorine–free paper.

ISBN 0-687-03541-4

All scripture quotations unless noted otherwise are taken from the *New Revised Standard Version of the Bible,* copyrighted 1989, Division of Christian Education of the National Council of the Churches of Christ in the United States of America. Used by permission. All rights reserved.

There may have been some changes in *Discipline* paragraph numbers or wording after this Guideline was printed. We regret any inconvenience.

MANUFACTURED IN THE UNITED STATES OF AMERICA

CONTENTS

4/Our Identity, Call, and Mission
6/"Small" Can Mean "Great Potential"
8/The Congregation's Mission
9/Achieving the Potential of Small Membership Churches
15/Organizing for Ministry: The NOW(rm) Model
19/Nurture Ministries
24/Outreach Ministries
29/Witness Ministries
36/Resource Ministries (rm)
39/Eight NOW(rm) Keys for Transforming Current Ministries
44/Resources

Julia Kuhn Wallace is Director of Small Membership Church and Shared Ministry at the General Board of Discipleship in Nashville, Tennessee. She has been active in smaller congregations for more than twenty years as a member, volunteer leader, educator, curriculum writer, consultant, and trainer. Current resources include the video: "Small Churches Can Make a Big Difference!", Vital Ministry in the Small Church Booklet Series (both available from Discipleship Resources) and the seminar "Vital Ministry in the Small Church: Making Disciples and Transforming Lives" (General Board of Discipleship).

She is married to a United Methodist pastor, Kenneth P. Wallace. They have raised their two children, Joshua and Amanda, in small membership churches where close relationships truly nurture the soul.

Ms. Wallace can be reached by phone: 877-899-2780 ext 7086, by e-mail: jwallace @gbod.org, or by fax: 615-340-7015. She welcomes your comments, questions, and experiences in small churches! Visit the Small Membership Church Web page at www.gbod.org.

Our Identity, Call, and Mission

About now a small voice in the back of your mind may be whispering, "What am I doing here? To what have I said yes? What is my role?" At the same time you may be aware that your congregation has extended to you a *call—a call to serve.* And you have said *yes—yes to leading in a vital mission.*

The mission of The United Methodist Church is to make disciples of Jesus Christ. You have agreed to serve as a leader bringing your unique passions, gifts, and abilities to the church. When the leaders focus on the church's purpose—*its mission of making disciples of Jesus Christ*—and link that purpose to the passions of the people, amazing things can happen.

The fundamental way we fulfill our mission is to reach out to people in the name of Jesus Christ, to relate people to God, to nurture and strengthen them in their journey of discipleship, and to send them into the world to be the church—inviting and receiving others in the name of Jesus Christ. We call this the primary task of The United Methodist Church. Effective leaders keep the whole of the primary task in their sight, working to keep all of its aspects in concert.

Leaders in the church must be first, and foremost, spiritual leaders who model and embrace Christian discipline and teaching. *By practicing the means of grace*—prayer, fasting, studying Scripture, corporate worship, celebration of the Lord's Supper, Christian conversation, and acts of mercy—*church leaders stay tuned to the mission of the church and live out the primary task.* Members and would-be members should be able to look to a congregation's leaders for spiritual example and direction because true leaders are known by their fruits. People's lives are changed through their influence.

Leaders use their gifts and talents to enable others to use their gifts and talents to the fullest potential. The flow of information, inspiration, guidance, and vision from leaders is an encouragement to others on their spiritual journey. Leaders help others to see new possibilities. When leaders are focused on the mission of the church, community is built and ministry occurs. The church focused on God is alive with creative energy aimed at transformation.

Four Essential Leadership Functions

Church leaders support and strengthen the church when they pay attention to these leadership functions: (1) help people discover the current reality in *which they live; (2) bring together the congregation's understandings of <u>current</u> reality and <u>desired</u> reality into a shared vision; (3) develop the plans to help the community move from current reality toward the reality of its shared vision; and finally, (4) monitor the whole work of the church as the congregation moves with God's guidance toward its vision.*

1. Discovering Current Reality

Accurately describing current reality—the way things are—may be the most important function of leadership. The booklets in this Guideline series offer suggestions for leaders to pay attention to the various committees of the church's ministry. In addition, it is critical for church leaders—lay and clergy—to spend time together discussing the ministry of the <u>whole</u> congregation. The conversation needs to include attentiveness to God's guidance and everything that describes a congregation's "what we are, here and now." Because God is always doing a new thing, this job is continuous. When we pay attention to change, we provide a base of integrity and strength from which to move into the future. Faith in Jesus Christ and a spiritual centering in God offers the strongest foundation to move people fearlessly through the massive changes of the twenty-first century.

2. Naming Shared Vision

Ask the question, "What do you want more than anything else in the world?" and most persons will give a response that indicates that they want to live in a world filled with love, faith, security, and meaning. Because persons desire a positive future, they are willing to invest themselves in organizations that are committed to it. By its very nature, the church is devoted to the creation of a better future. When the church promises to move people personally and corporately toward their desired reality, people will invest time, energy, and resources into the church. As people see their own desires linked to the congregational vision and a deeper understanding of God's future, they deepen their commitment and involvement. Building this link is a vital role of leadership.

Naming a shared vision is accomplished by asking people about their lives and their faith, and by listening very carefully. By listening, we mean deep listening—the kind that requires setting aside our own agendas and entering into the worldviews of others, and listening for God through the conversation. It is a significant shift in our understanding of leadership in the church to move from telling people what we think they need to know to listening to people in order to find out who they are and what their desired realities are. Effective spiritual leaders listen to the hearts of people and begin to articulate a shared vision.

3. Developing Bridges

To span the gulf between our current reality and the hope expressed in the shared vision, leaders must build a bridge. The third critical function of leadership is to plan actions and develop systems that create the bridge across this gulf. Leaders who are elected to administrative and program committees are responsible for the ongoing work of the church and must pay attention to the present. At the same time, leaders *must* be focused on the future—keeping today and tomorrow in tension—ensuring that the church does not get stuck in the past, present, or future.

Church leaders who are attentive to God's leading and who can hold the tension between today and tomorrow are *visionary leaders*. Visionary leaders see it all—current reality, desired reality, and the bridges to get from one to the other.

4. Monitoring the Journey

Perhaps the most critical task for leaders is keeping an eye on the whole of the faith journey of the congregation. When leaders are constantly caught up in "doing" the administrative and program work of the church, there is not any time left for "being" with God in prayer to discern the leading of the Spirit for the congregation. Leaders must step back from "doing" constant activities in order to pay attention to the total direction of the church's mission and ministry. All elected and appointed leaders must spend time together listening to God in prayer, Bible study, conversation, and other means of grace in order to lead the entire community in the work of Christ. Anything less is not Christian spiritual leadership.

"Small" Can Mean "Great Potential"

What happens when you put the words "small" and "church" together? Do you think of the family of God? A style of ministry that is relational? *A ministry with great potential?*

A small membership church is not a "miniature" large church—*a small membership church is distinctive both in style and potential.* Small membership churches are important because they are involved in the vital and very significant work of making disciples. Just as God once lifted up the tiny nation of Israel to be a witness, God still calls the small congregation to do the same today. Throughout out the Bible we discover that a faithful and successful ministry does not depend on large numbers. The writer of Deuteronomy says:

> It was not because you were more numerous than any other people that the LORD set his heart on you and chose you—for you were the fewest of all peoples. It was because the Lord loved you and kept the oath that he swore to your ancestors. (Deuteronomy 7:7a)

This Guideline is designed to help:
- You to be a more effective leader of your small membership church;
- Your leadership team understand the church's mission of making disciples and work together in fulfilling that vital mission;
- You formulate a clear vision of what God is calling your small membership church to be and to do for the sake of the gospel of Jesus Christ;
- You organize your congregation's resources for service in your local church, your community, and the world;
- Your small membership church recognize its potential.

Churches with Special Qualities

Leaders participating in a seminar on ministry of small membership churches listed qualities that are specific to the small church: close, caring relationships; intergenerational education and fellowship that resembles a family; mentoring youth and children in the faith; knowing people by name; quick response to crisis and disaster; generosity of spirit; offering individuals a place to be involved in meaningful ministry; and a deep sense of stewardship that connects with environmental issues and concerns. Churches with small membership numbers are often dynamically involved in their communities (and even in the world) through ministries of nurture, outreach, and witness. *These churches are making a difference—they matter!*

What would you say about the ministry of *your* church? *Is it a vital, dynamic ministry?*

*Editor's Note: **In the interest of space, "small membership church" and "small church" will be used interchangeably, but it is with the clear understanding that "small" is in reference only to numbers—not in terms of spirit or potential.***

Small membership churches are everywhere: in rural, inner-city, urban, suburban, ex-urban, small town, or open country locations. The populations they serve may be stable, growing, aging, or even in the midst of transition. Limits to numerical growth often depend on factors beyond a church's control, such as the demographic setting (a declining, steady, growing or changing population base), economics, and environment. Sometimes there are other internal factors that have inhibited growth that need to be resolved, such as rapid pastoral turnover and not providing adequate hospitality to visitors.

Your small membership church may never become a large membership congregation. It can, however, learn to do effective ministry by making the very best use of the resources with which it has been blessed by God. Look at where you are strategically placed to reach people who live or work all around you! Are you effectively reaching out to people and offering them Christ?

Size and Style

A small membership church can be defined as one that has less than 200 members (or fewer than 150 in worship attendance). But size alone does not define or limit the small church. Ministry in small membership churches can better be described in terms of style. *"Family" is the word most used to describe the small church.* Family implies close relationships and bonds. People matter.

In churches with worship attendance under 50, the group (or family) is the primary unit. This church tends to do many things together: worship, study, and serve others. Laity serve as key leaders who serve as guiding parents (matriarchs or patriarchs), and they are often expected to make key decisions. Instead of an administrative role, the pastor has a more priestly function that guides the spiritual life of the congregation.

In the family church it is important to work as a family with mutual respect for each person. Laity may feel overwhelmed by responsibilities; clergy may feel as if they are "sidelined."

The church with worship attendance between 51 and 150 still functions like a family, with two distinct differences: pastoral leadership is central in a core of lay leadership, and smaller groups become functional for study and service. Fellowship is still of utmost importance.

In today's society with broken and dysfunctional families, there is yearning for a sense of home with people who care deeply for one another. The small church can be the place where people discover that God cares! Small churches are known for their networks of caring that extend out into the community and into the world.

The Congregation's Mission

Regardless of size, each congregation is called to be a community of Christian people organized to carry out God's mission for the church as defined in Matthew 28:19–20. "Go into all the world and make

disciples, baptizing and teaching them all that I have taught you."
Accomplishing the mission of making disciples requires:
- Reaching out into the world surrounding the congregation and joyfully receiving into the family of faith all who would respond;
- Encouraging people in their relationship with God and inviting them into a commitment to God's love in Jesus Christ;
- Providing opportunities for people to be nurtured and to practice the disciplines of faith;
- Supporting people to live and act as faithful disciples in ministry to the world in the power of the Holy Spirit.

This statement is referred to as the "Primary Task of the Congregation." It defines the essential process to be carried out if the congregation is to be faithful!

Achieving the Potential of Small Membership Churches

There are many small churches that actively proclaim their faith in God by the amazing things they do in God's name: raising more money than their annual budget for mission; running a volunteer emergency response team; feeding the hungry in their area; caring for the sick; offering a hospice ministry; or tutoring children to read. For these churches, ministry is the embodiment of Christ active in the world. What do the ministries of your church proclaim to the world around you?

The list of creative ministries in small membership congregations is not defined by numbers or resources, but by the capacity to reach beyond the congregation and care for others. Small churches that have big hearts have a huge capacity to serve God and neighbor in practical, relevant ways.

In essence, a small church can still do great things in the name of Jesus Christ! Despite small numbers or even limited resources, your church has an important job to do! *Size may guide "how" you go about it; it does not offer an excuse.*

Measures of the Effective Small Church
Several factors can influence the effectiveness of your church's ministry, but vision and prayer are crucial.

Vision
Vision and purpose mean simply to yearn for God's desire. As a church our vision is not hindsight or based on the past—it pulls us together today and leads us into tomorrow. Because the small church cannot (and should not)

try to do everything, it must discern the right thing to do and then do it to the very best of its ability! Vision provides a compass or map for the journey of a people seeking God's kingdom. Vision in the church is always directly related to the mission of making disciples.

A clear vision of purpose linked to ministry goals designed to accomplish that vision is necessary if the church is to have an effective ministry. So, what is God's desire for you? For your church? For your community?

Use your strengths. Small churches are not only vital, they are also important to God's purpose for the world. These communities of faith offer two unique strengths to people who would be disciples of Jesus Christ: a sense of *intimacy* (place of belonging) and *involvement* in meaningful ministry (place of service).

1. *Developing a keen sense of intimacy means being a place of belonging.* A healthy small church calls people by name. In larger churches it may be possible to attend worship regularly and never hear your name called out by another. In smaller congregations, your name is not only known, it is also respected. People new to a community (or newly seeking the faith) can find a place of deep caring in a smaller congregation. One of the benchmarks of a vital small church is how far the fellowship and caring extends. Many times it goes beyond the active membership to those who live, work, and struggle in the community. Who does your church welcome and call by name? Who is excluded? Why?
2. *Involving others in meaningful ministry means offering a place of service that matters.* Not only does the small church call you by name, it also calls you "gifted." Because people are special to God and gifted by God for ministry, a healthy small church works hard at identifying, nurturing, and utilizing the gifts, talents, and resources of people. In a small church each and every person is necessary in completing God's purpose. Small churches need to be careful stewards of the gifts of each person so that people feel needed as they are invited to participate in ministry. Another benchmark of a vital small church is how well it shares leadership and ministry with one another! Do you spend more time in meetings than you do in ministry? How can you free up more time to be used in Christian service? Are the same people always doing the activities of the church, or are there new faces sharing new ways of being effective? How do the members of your church share the work of ministry with one another?

Prayer
People in a strong and vital small church pray! The writer of the Letter to the Hebrews concludes (13:18–19) with the reminder that Christian leaders

need one another's prayers to surmount the difficulties and challenges of their work. Without this mutual prayer support, it is easy to succumb to discouragement and sin.

Not only should the congregation be praying for its ministries, it should also be praying for individuals and their relationship to God. For example, one small membership church has several "prayer warriors" who arrive twenty to thirty minutes before the worship service. They sit quietly in the sanctuary and pray that God will bless the pastor, the choir, and other worship leaders during the service. They also pray that God will help any visitors to the service find the meaning and direction they need for life and faith. Several choir members and Sunday School teachers, who are busy just before the worship service, also offer similar prayers at 8:00 on Sunday mornings. Since this program was instituted, that congregation has seen a remarkable growth in its worship attendance and its vitality.

While anonymity is essential, it is nevertheless necessary that members of small churches regularly pray and request prayers for persons who have not professed faith in Jesus Christ. Often, a person who prays in this manner will discover natural and appropriate ways to share his or her faith with others or to provide needed acts of kindness to them. These opportunities become channels for witnessing ministries and help truly mobilize the church's witness ministries. There is no substitute for praying for the church's ministries—it is where all ministries should begin.

Use the Appropriate Variety of Styles and Pastoral Service

Despite a similar call to mission, no two congregations live out that call in quite the same way. Context or setting, theological expression, and discerning effective ministry offer unique opportunities to be the body of Christ. There are many equally valuable and valid ways to be the church today.

Some churches are formed around a single faith community. This style of church may be a station or charge that has one pastor and one place of worship. Other churches are composed of several faith communities. Some small churches (and some medium- and large-size churches, too) have found new vitality by forming partnerships with other area churches to share ministry cooperatively. The goal of cooperative ministries is simple: to do together what you cannot do effectively alone. Cooperative ministry does not take the place of being an individual church, rather it supplements a church's mission and ministry. That is, *cooperative ministry means doing those things together that cannot be done alone, and doing together those things that can be done better in partnership than alone.*

Ten different forms of cooperative ministry are defined in *The Book of Discipline,* 2000 (¶206.3). They range from informal to formal relationships. Because each style is unique and has implications for how the cooperative ministry is formed, they should be examined and chosen carefully.

Formal cooperative ministries include the multiple charge cooperative parish, group ministry, cluster group, probe/exploration staff, federated church, and ecumenical cooperative parish. *Informal cooperative ministries* include sharing facilities with another congregation, sharing ministry projects (such as youth or VBS), a collective or covenant (several congregations who strive together to serve the community needs), a mission or new church (started by another congregation to serve a specific area or group).

Because of the options of a variety of styles and contexts for ministry, discerning the form is a critical task for smaller congregations. While economic realities, congregational membership, and other constraints sometimes drive the decision to form a certain style of church, *effectively serving the community in the name of Jesus Christ should be the primary motivation.*

In addition to the variety of congregational arrangements, there are many options for appointing pastoral leadership. Some churches are served by one pastor; others share a pastor. Some churches that have more than one place of worship also have more than one clergy to serve as pastor. Some pastors are elders who have gone through seminary and have been ordained by their Annual Conference. Some pastors are "licensed" as local pastors. Some may be second career pastors who bring many gifts to ministry. Some ministers are bivocational pastors—they serve a church less than full time and also serve the community in another profession such as being a nurse, lawyer, teacher, dairy farmer, and so on. Sometimes laity are invited to serve as pastor—they may be certified lay speakers with pastoral gifts. People consecrated for ministry, such as deacons, may also be appointed to serve a church. The range of pastoral options also includes student pastors and semiretired pastors.

What type of pastoral leadership is best for your church? One way to answer that question is with another question. Is your church growing, either numerically or spiritually? If the answer is yes, then your current pastoral leadership may be adequate. If the answer is no, then it is possible that your current form of pastoral leadership is providing just enough guidance for your church to remain stable or, unfortunately, so little leadership that your church is declining. It takes commitment on the part of church and district leadership to discern the appropriate style of church and pastoral leadership.

Small churches that wish to grow spiritually or numerically should annually review their form of pastoral leadership with their district superintendent. Focus more on the abilities of the pastor than the style. The United Methodist Church needs pastors who are:
- Growing spiritually themselves and have a heart for God;
- Excited or passionate about vital ministry;
- Knowledgeable about United Methodist Church polity and theology;
- Committed to mission and outreach;
- Organized and willing to plan for ministry;
- Team players who respect the laity;
- Willing to develop shared ministries.

The small church is a place for service! Pastoral leaders should serve as spiritual leaders appointed to work with people in the church and community to discern God's will.

Awareness of the Meaning of Ministry

"It's not my job—it's the preacher's!" may be a common refrain in some churches. Participants in a recent seminar for leaders in small churches were invited to stand in the center of the room if they believed they were called to full-time Christian service. Only the clergy moved to the center. Where was everybody else? Why?

By our very baptism, we are each called a child of God—gifted by God for the work of ministry. The work is full-time for all of us. Some are called to be pastors, others are called as laity. Small churches with effective ministries realize that while it is important to have a caring and competent pastor, *all Christians are called to be ministers!*

Building Relationships that Matter

Relationships are crucial in the small church. In fact, the strength of the small church depends on the strength of its relationships. There are four relationships, or partnerships, that can make or break the church with small membership. These relationships can be viewed as connections:

1. *God Connections:* Just as God is to be worshiped and praised, God is to be the life center in the congregation. Whenever we come together as a church, God is in our midst. When we worship, attend Sunday School or a small group, participate in a service project, or do anything that centers on the sacred, we seek to grow in the knowledge, grace, and will of God.

How strong is this connection in your church? Where are the avenues for people of all ages to grow spiritually? Are worship and Christian education prime times or pastimes? As a leader in the church, what are the ways in which you personally participate in the means of grace and grow spiritually?

2. *Leadership Connections:* A congregation that is growing closer to God's purpose has individuals who are doing the same. Men and women who come together for ministry tasks and who respect, trust, and depend on each another form an awesome team. A team is a group of people who understand that they can accomplish far more working together than they can alone. Christian church leaders understand that one of their responsibilities is to mentor and encourage one another in the faith and in developing leadership skills. Leadership has little to do with controlling the decisions or actions of others.

How well do people in leadership positions work together to accomplish ministry? Who makes the key decisions? How? Is more time spent in meetings than in ministry? Are people eager or reluctant to serve as leaders in the church?

3. *Congregation Connections:* If at its best, the small church is a family whose members care deeply for each another, *then the strength of this connection is in the depth of caring.*

How does your church rate on this connection? Is there a place for everyone at your church family table? How long does it take to be accepted in your church? If someone has a need, how and when does your church respond? Are there people who are "out," or is everyone "in"? How does your church resolve conflict or difference of opinion?

4. *Community Connections:* Sometimes it seems like the best kept secret in the community is the church, but the effective church relates to the community.

How would your church answer the following? How well is your church known in the community around it? What quality service is your church known for providing? How does your church communicate ministry to people beyond its membership? What groups or people outside your church are respected partners to accomplish projects and meet needs?

These four connections remind us that no church is called to serve itself. Small churches that are growing have leaders who pray for each another, learn together, serve together, and share ministry with one another. When these connections are balanced, so is ministry!

Perseverance

Making these connections stronger takes patience—they are not forged overnight. You have got to care about each another and the community you serve! Perhaps there is a need for forgiveness and reconciliation between two individuals or groups. Perhaps an intentional focus on strengthening these connections on the part of every church leader is needed. Some church leaders develop a covenant that makes these connections the central focus of their ministry.

Communication

One pastor saw the potential for an after-school ministry with neighborhood children. He met with the leadership council and presented the idea. They agreed to give it a try and use Sunday school space. Eventually the program grew to have thirty-five children! Four months later, the children's class teacher resigned in tears. Each Sunday when she came to church to teach, her supplies and furniture were in disarray. She spent more time straightening the room than teaching the children Bible! No one had explained to her that the "after-school" would share space with her Sunday school class. She never had an opportunity to meet with the after-school teacher and work out the arrangements.

Clear communication strategies help strengthen our connections with one another. Sometimes people within the church, or even around it, lack the clarity of purpose to understand a church goal or activity so they can fully participate. How do your church leaders communicate ministry opportunities and key decisions so that others can fully understand and support them?

Understanding the Culture

In a rapidly changing world, diversity (such as multicultural membership) demands an awareness that there are a number of ways to look at something and respond. Sensitivity to difference is a must for successful collaboration. There are many resources available to help congregations successfully work with groups of different cultural backgrounds (see "Resources").

Organizing for Ministry: The NOW(rm) Model

The purpose of organizing for ministry is not simply to plan activities that fill up a calendar and exhausts us. A small church should never fall into the trap of substituting "busyness" (activity) for business (spiritual formation). The "bigger is better" mentality does not support the development and implementation of ministry in the small membership church. It is a matter of wisdom—choosing the right things and doing them well.

The United Methodist Church affirms three specific areas of ministry for local United Methodist churches—*nurture, outreach,* and *mission*—that provide a way of organizing ministry which is helpful for congregations of every size. We call this way of organizing ministry NOW (for *nurture, outreach,* and *witness*). The name alone encourages faithful ministry responses in the present.

Nurture, outreach, witness ministries depend on organized *resource ministries* (rm) in the local church. *Resource ministries include the support that four groups in the church provide*: trustees, finance, pastor (staff) parish, and nominations and personnel. Together these emphases provide for the administration of the church's organizational and temporal life. (*The Book of Discipline* ¶251).

NOW and its resource ministries (rm) are summarized as ***NOW(rm)***. NOW(rm) is based on biblical foundations, current realities and possibilities, and needs. Utilizing the NOW(rm) model for ministry can help your congregation effectively balance its life as a dynamic community of faith.

The work of organizing and administrating the church's ministries always requires careful planning, implementation, and evaluation. However, the administration and organization of the church's ministries is never an end in itself, rather it must be seen as the means to the actual ministries of the church.

NOW(rm) Offers Options for Organizing

NOW(rm) provides a variety of options for organizing church ministries. Regardless of which organizational system you adopt or invent, it is imperative that your church (1) *take a close look at its own current situation,* (2) *develop its own vision of the future,* and then (3) *decide its own avenues for ministry and its own organizational system.* In doing this with the guidance of the Holy Spirit, the church will have the flexibility and the freedom to truly "reinvent" itself.

NOW(rm) can suggest means of organizing that can become as elaborate as necessary, but organization can also be quite simple. Some small churches, particularly those with an average worship attendance of less than twenty-five persons, simply do not have enough members to form committees. These churches function with one organizing group, the church council.

Churches in this category, however, can still use the NOW(rm) model by having a single ministry group person responsible for each of the ministries of nurture, outreach, and witness. Thus, when the church council meets, for the time devoted to planning nurture (outreach or witness) ministries, the church council itself can serve as the committee for nurture (outreach or witness) ministries. The key is in placing primary emphasis on the ministries of nurture, outreach, and witness while understanding that the various resource ministries exist only to support the NOW ministries, not as ends in themselves.

Three Necessary Keys

There are three important keys to designing successful ministries using NOW(rm):

Leadership Commitment

People who make the ministry decisions in the church must support a common understanding of being in ministry, and they must commit themselves toward working together to its success. They must be trained and encouraged. *NOW(rm) is not about doing things right—it is more a matter of doing the right things.* A dynamic church must do more than simply nurture the people who come into the building—it must reach beyond itself and live out its discipleship. Leadership commitment must expand to more than the task of balancing nurture, outreach, witness, and resource ministries. It must also be a commitment to journey together. This happens when leaders know, respect, and trust each other, when leaders understand and name what the church expects of them as well as what they offer the church.

Assessment of Current Ministry and Needs

Honestly review the needs and activities of people or groups in the church and community who are truly being served. Successful leaders discern where the place of greatest potential is for ministry. Leaders who truly know the community (through demographic studies, "pounding the pavement," interviews, informal conversations, and so on) are ready to respond to those decisive moments that may open a spiritual doorway for someone seeking a deeper faith experience. Does the church do an equal job of taking care of those outside the church and those within? Are nurture ministries balanced carefully with outreach and witness? Is the church focused more on maintenance than mission? Does the leadership know where the unchurched live and what they need in order to respond to the gospel? Is survival or service the deciding factor on what happens in the church, how it is done, and with whom?

> Meet together with other leaders in your church and discuss the following questions:
> - What is the membership of your congregation? Who are the people in attendance? What is the average worship attendance of your congregation? What is the average Sunday school attendance of your congregation? Are the answers to these questions acceptable to you? Why or why not?
> - When you think about your church, what images come to mind? How are these images affected by your size? Is this positive or negative? Why do you think this way? When the rest of your congregation thinks about your church, what do they think about first: its size or the fact that it is a Christian church? In what way does your congregation's thinking impact the faith, self-esteem, and actions of its members as individual Christians?

Creativity: Willing to Risk and Try Something New

Sometimes the patterns of ministry can become our prison. The more successful past ministries are in our minds and hearts, the more powerful they can be in controlling the present and ultimately the future. We do the same activities in the same way year after year (and wonder why we are not getting the same response we once did). Vain traditions make void the living Word of God. A new day often demands a new faithful response. Is there a way to honor traditions *and* people's needs/expectations at the same time? Do new ideas thrive or die in your church?

Remember that your church needs to be willing to take some risks. Some of your efforts will produce growth, while others may not be as productive. Do not waste time dwelling on the latter. Learn from both your successes and mistakes. Move on.

As you set goals for nurture, outreach, witness, and resource ministries, it is important to do regular evaluation. The traditional concept of the Wesleyan quarterly conferences is one way to do this. The church council should review its annual goals quarterly to see which goals have been accomplished and which are still in need of implementation. One church publishes for the entire congregation a quarterly report of its annual goals and their progress. Much to their surprise, they have discovered that such methodical attention to detail usually results in their having achieved most of their annual goals in the first six months of the year. This gives them the second half of the year to work on the quality of their service plus plan for the next year.

> Questions for leadership reflection:
> - What vision for ministry was expressed by your church's founders? How has that vision changed over the years? What is your congregation's vision for its ministry today? Is that vision adequate for the present? Why or why not?
> - What do you think God wants for your church? How are you moving toward that hope?
> - What does the Bible and church tradition tell you about leadership?
>
> By exploring these questions faithfully, you may begin to glimpse the power that balancing ministry with the NOW(rm) approach offers your church for vitality and renewal.

Nurture Ministries

People need a growing relationship with Jesus Christ and the Christian community. "Nurture" identifies the need for Christians to be nurtured in the Christian faith if they are to cultivate the spiritual resources necessary to provide effective outreach and witness ministries. Here is the task force's definition of nurture ministries:

> Nurture and fellowship focus largely on the internal needs of a congregation and prepare the people of that church for ministry outside their congregation within the context of their community and world. (Report of the Strengthening the Church with Small Membership Task Force to the 1992 General Conference)

The Book of Discipline defines the work of nurturing ministries as giving attention to *educational, worship*, and *stewardship* components of ministry.

Biblical Basis: While the entire Bible tells the story of God's nurturing love for humanity, Jesus Christ is God's nurturing love made flesh. We know that in addition to Jesus' call to his disciples to follow him, he also nurtured them. He taught them what they needed to know so that they could grow in faith. For example, one of the disciples asked Jesus how they should pray, and he taught them what we know as the Lord's Prayer (Luke 11:1–4).

However, Jesus did not stop with teaching about prayer. His daily conversations with the disciples and his followers were filled with instructions about faith in God. He also tenderly took care of his disciples, identifying with the shepherds who tended sheep (John 10:11–18). We often think of Jesus as offering spiritual food to his disciples. However, on at least one occasion Jesus prepared a much needed meal for his closest disciples (John 21:1–14).

Jesus was intimately involved in the care of his disciples. He made sure they had enough to eat. He calmed the storm when it threatened to drown them. However, he did more than just take care of his flock. He challenged his followers to become disciples. He taught them the hard lessons of discipleship, constantly reminding them of the power of the ancient Scriptures while further illuminating those words through instruction. And through teaching the importance of baptism and the Eucharist, Jesus nurtured the disciples in the healing and empowering presence of the Holy Spirit.

Nurture Ministries Are Expressed in Many Ways

Activities like Sunday School, visitation of the sick and those who find it difficult to leave home, and the worship program of the congregation come to mind first when we think about nurture. However, it is helpful to remember that the church's nurturing ministries are much broader than just two or three programs.

The educational ministry of the church, for instance, incorporates the Sunday school program and may include other opportunities for Christian education, such as Bible studies, prayer groups, and short-term classes. Short-term classes can address a variety of needs in the congregation, from instruction on Christian parenting, to care of the elderly, and even congregational conflict management. The educational program of the church can also include leadership training for church officers and Sunday School leaders and teachers.

Perhaps the most urgently needed type of nurturing ministry today is simply *assisting members of the congregation in their daily walk of faith.* Persons who seek to grow in faith are people who are constantly assailed by a variety of activities that compete for their time and energy. Growing disciples need help in developing habits that include daily Scripture reading, praying, and listening to God.

Fellowship, another type of nurture activity, should be designed to meet the needs of everyone in the congregation. Events should be planned that meet the needs of families, older persons, single persons, children, and youth and should include those who feel discriminated against or marginalized by society. Sometimes this can be accomplished through intergenerational activities. At other times a particular group of folks in the congregation may find mutual support by spending time with each other.

Members of a congregation need to know that others in the church care about them. One important way to care for each other is to pray for each other. Lending a helping hand—when someone is sick, ill, or injured; or when a baby is born; or when a loved one dies—is another way to demonstrate care and love. Although overlooked in many churches, having fun together (fellowship) is another way to provide joyous emotional support to all members of the congregation.

The Sunday worship service is an important vehicle for nurturing the congregation. Care should be taken to plan worship that appeals to everyone in the congregation, realizing that no one can be pleased all the time. In general, the more the members of the congregation have an opportunity to plan and participate in the worship services, the more meaningful these services are for them. Overall, the worship program of the church should be inspirational and spiritually stimulating.

Educational Nurture Ministries
1. Short-term (2 to 12 weeks) Christian education study classes for adults
2. Disciple Bible Study
3. Spiritual Gifts Discovery classes
4. Annual church board/council retreats
5. Ongoing or short-term Bible study or Covenant Discipleship groups
6. Vacation Bible school for children and/or adults
7. Lenten and Advent studies
8. Developing seasonal devotions to use in the home
9. Confirmation and membership classes
9. Training programs for Sunday school and Vacation Bible school teachers
10. Developing a booklet designed to inform church members and friends about the congregation's history, structure, programs, and so forth
11. Afterschool programs for children and youth (Pathways or Logos)
12. Choir rehearsals that also include the study of the Bible and church hymns
13. Rites of passage experiences for youth

(Note that several of the above are a type of discipling nurture ministry.)

Fellowship Nurture Ministries
1. Offering hospitality training for worship greeters and key leaders
2. United Methodist Men
3. United Methodist Women
4. United Methodist Youth
5. Midweek evening program for children and families
6. Afterschool or Saturday care programs for children (like Kid's Club)

7. Church camp scholarships
8. Intergenerational activities
9. Children's day camp or summer camp

Physical and Emotional Support Nurture Ministries
1. Being supportive of one another
2. Providing wheelchairs and other equipment so that people who need them can have access to nurture ministries
3. Good financial stewardship (which provides for the church facilities and paid staff)
4. Leadership training and prayer support
5. Sending cards and devotional material, such as the *Upper Room,* to the homebound
6. Pastoral ministries, such as Stephen Ministry, that involve laity in listening and caring for others
7. Provide meals for individuals and families going through tough times

Worship Nurture Ministries
1. A monthly lectionary study for people who want to help plan and participate as worship leaders
2. Special music for worship services (children's choir, special selections, spirited singing involving a new instrument (such as guitar, synthesizer, drums)
3. Dramas and short skits
4. Special Sundays (social, such as Mother's Day; denominational celebrations, such as Native American Awareness Sunday; and Christian Education Day
5. Involvement of various people in worship services utilized in a variety of ways
6. Special worship services, such as Thanksgiving, Good Friday, Easter Sunrise
7. Ecumenical worship celebrations, such as Church Women United World Day of Prayer
8. Fifth Sunday Charge Worship and Fellowship Dinner
9. Spiritual Life Retreats or Days Apart

These lists are not meant to be exhaustive. What would you add?

Use the following questions to help you discern your church's unique ministries that nurture people and help them grow spiritually.
1. Below you will find some synonyms for the word *nurture:*

aid	assistance	comfort
cure	help	feed
support	nourish	protect
care	raise	assist

> What stories of Jesus' life come to mind as you read these words? How has Jesus nurtured your life? How have you felt yourself nurtured by other Christians?
>
> 2. Is there a difference between taking care of a congregation and making disciples? If so, what?

Organize and Assess Your Church's Nurture Ministries

Forming a team of people who will work on developing nurture ministries is important. Even small churches should have more than one person working in this area. A representative from nurture should be on the church leadership council. Begin by asking the following questions:

1. How does your church nurture its members to become disciples of Jesus Christ?

2. In which area do you think your church is strongest: nurture, outreach, or witness? Why?

3. Inventory the nurture ministries that are taking place at your church. You may wish to categorize them as follows:

    a. Educational

    b. Fellowship

    c. Providing physical and emotional support

    d. Worship

   How do these ministries help persons become and grow as disciples? If you wish, you may also list the nurturing ministries provided by your pastor and, if available, other paid staff. List your nurture ministries on newsprint and/or in minutes. Save your list for future reference.

4. What specific nurture needs not currently being met does your congregation have in the following areas?

Small Membership Church

- Educational
- Fellowship
- Physical and emotional care and support for persons of all ages, including the elderly
- Worship
- Pastoral ministry
- Development of disciples

5. Think about what God might be calling you to do so that each member of your congregation feels loved and supported and so that everyone can grow in faith. Dream a little! What new nurture ministries should you add to the ones already being accomplished at your church?

Outreach Ministries

United Methodist churches of all sizes are called to provide outreach ministries on the local, state, regional, national, and international levels. However, doing outreach ministries on the local level is often a way to initially involve folks in this type of ministry. The following information is provided to help your church determine how it can most effectively provide outreach ministries on the local level.

To provide outreach ministries appropriate for your community, you need to analyze the needs of your community. One way to do this is to interview persons in your community who are aware of these needs. These may include, but are not limited to, the following: public school nurse, police chief, senior citizens center director, fire department chief, county/regional social service director, county/regional health director, community organizing project director, and others who serve the community. Questions you should ask these persons include the following:
- Who are the people with needs in this community?
- What do they need?
- Are there different kinds of needs?
- How can the church respond to these needs?

Be Bold. "Because of God's abundant grace, there is never anything inherently small about any church!" This proclamation tells us that while some tasks may seem enormous, the infinite availability of God's grace makes it possible for a church of any size to address these tasks. The church with a small membership may not be able to do everything, but it can do something!

Just as the inward vision of the church with a small membership must address the needs of all its members, the outward vision must address the needs of the church's local, state, national, and international neighbors. Outreach ministries may take expression in several forms:

Ministries of compassion involve a congregation in addressing the immediate needs of individuals, families, and communities. The congregation may respond to local disasters and/or provide food, clothing, emergency housing, counseling, employment opportunities, and so forth in their community.

Community ministries of concern and advocacy call for a congregation's involvement in the enrichment of community life and advocacy for justice—changes in local communities related to welfare, long-term housing, education, community economic development, health services, and so on.

Regional, national, and global outreach ministries call on a congregation to engage the structures and values of society and to move toward justice and righteousness in public policies, such as basic human rights, land use and control, ecology, and the world's economic systems.

The Book of Discipline (¶251.2.b) defines the work of the outreach ministries as follows:

> The outreach ministries . . . shall give attention to the local and larger community ministries of compassion, justice and advocacy. These ministries include church and society, global ministries, higher education and campus ministry, health and welfare, Christian unity and interreligious concerns, religion and race, and the status and role of women.

Biblical Basis: Many of the best loved stories of the Scriptures portray Jesus and his disciples caring for the immediate needs of people. Jesus feeding the multitudes (Matthew 14:13–21) and Peter and John healing a man in Jesus' name (Acts 3:1–8) are examples of the ministries of compassion. In John 21:15–19 the risen Christ has a poignant conversation with Peter. In this conversation Jesus repeatedly instructs Peter to "feed my sheep," thus underscoring the importance of responding to the needs of persons who suffer from hurt and want. Who in your community suffers from hurt and want?

However, Jesus' concern was not just with the needs of individuals. Jesus wept over the entire population of Jerusalem (Luke 19:41–44), he sent his disciples to a multitude of towns (Luke 10:1), and he devoted himself to healing the sick in the region of Gennesaret (Mark 6:53–56). It is obvious from these passages that Jesus was concerned with communities. By his own example Jesus taught his disciples how to address the needs of entire cities, towns, and villages.

Jesus' ministry also addressed the systemic evils that impacted the lives of people. His teaching that Samaritans, the traditional enemies of the Jewish people, could be perceived as good (Luke 10:25–37) and his open relationships with women (Mark 3:31–35; Matthew 12:46–50; and Luke 8:19–21) are examples of Jesus' willingness to overturn the restrictive social patterns of his time. Jesus saw the effects of greed upon the communities he visited, and he proclaimed a new ecology of living based on the sustainable use of resources (Matthew 6:25-32). Jesus' life and teachings caused the apostle Paul to proclaim that with the coming of Jesus there was no longer any validity to racism, classism, or sexism (Galatians 3:28).

Outreach Ministries Through Giving Plus

Many churches with small membership are doing needed and exciting outreach ministries of compassion. One traditional way of doing this in United Methodist churches is by supporting United Methodist missional and benevolence apportionments. United Methodist apportionments help fund outreach ministries in local and annual conference settings, as well as in the fifty states of the USA and in more than 108 countries.

With few exceptions, small membership churches can pay 100 percent of their apportionments. Clergy and lay leadership in these churches need to find creative ways to inform the congregation about how these apportionments are used in ministry. One way to do this is to have a "Church in Action" report during worship (monthly or weekly) in which a short summary of outreach (missional) work is presented. It is also important to provide opportunities to celebrate this missional giving and its results.

Doing outreach ministries includes more than simply giving dollars; congregation members should be encouraged *to do* outreach ministries. A hands-on experience, such as working on a Habitat for Humanity construction project or serving food in a soup kitchen, can often bring a sense of satisfaction and accomplishment that far outweighs placing a donation in the offering plate. Hands-on outreach ministries also provide opportunities for church members to reconnect experientially to their local community, nation, and world.

Effective churches with a small membership both support and do outreach ministries. They also embrace John Wesley's belief that the world is their parish. That is, they see the need to provide outreach ministries on the following levels:
1. Local community
2. State, regional, and national
3. International

Sometimes members of the congregation resist supporting outreach ministries on the international level, stating that they prefer "to take care of their own people first." People who express this sentiment should be reminded that we all live on a very small planet in a large solar system located in an even larger galaxy that is part of an infinite universe. God calls all of us who live on this tiny "global village" to reach out to one another with ministries that help and heal.

Examples of Outreach Ministries

> These ideas are intended to generate the development of outreach ministries in your church rather than to serve as a grab bag for activity.

Ministries of Compassion
1. Giving child care scholarships to young mothers in the community to help them complete high school
2. Providing free funeral dinners to nonmembers
3. Collecting an "ABLE" fund (Aid Beyond Legal Extent) for emergency situations where people are displaced from their homes
4. Volunteering to deliver Meals on Wheels
5. Providing emergency financial aid: utilities, food, clothing, shelter, medicine
6. Doing errands for older persons and providing transportation to doctor appointments
7. Serving as Hospice volunteers (providing support to the terminally ill and their families)
8. Serving as an emergency medical technician or fire department volunteer
9. Organizing a clothing thrift shop or emergency food shelter
10. Making quilts to give to impoverished families, victims of natural disasters, and so forth
11. Cooking and serving a Thanksgiving dinner for people who are homeless or home alone
12. Gleaning fruits and vegetables for low-income households
13. Holding rockathons, walkathons, fun runs, and so forth to raise money for world ministries and missions
14. Receiving special offerings in response to natural disasters
15. Making contributions to General Advance Special missions projects
16. Sponsoring mission fairs that use games, bake sales, and so forth to raise funds, while also providing displays about outreach
17. Sponsoring a Job Fair and inviting community employers

Community Ministries of Concern and Advocacy

1. Donating seeds, fertilizers, and canning equipment to low-income households and teaching them how to garden, can, and freeze foods
2. Financially supporting and raising breeder stock for the Heifer Project International, which provides animals and related assistance to poor rural families and communities to enable them to produce food and income on a long-term basis
3. Sponsoring work camps designed to improve substandard housing, construct church camp buildings, and so forth
4. Befriending local drug addicts for the purpose of showing them the love of Christ and encouraging them to seek treatment for their addiction
5. Providing funds and labor for Habitat for Humanity, an organization that constructs low-cost housing for impoverished people in both urban and rural areas
6. Hosting work trips to mission sites in the United States, Mexico, and Latin America
7. Financially supporting and volunteering to help with local domestic violence assistance programs
8. Paying the cost for a reading teacher in the local elementary school, or volunteering as tutors
9. Volunteering at senior centers or other places in your community that serve a population group
10. Developing a response team to the Bishop's Initiative on Children and Poverty
11. Gathering perishables for holiday food baskets
12. Supporting or hosting a refugee or immigrant family in your area

Regional, National, and Global Outreach

1. Going on a Volunteers in Missions trip
2. Being a part of a disaster response team
3. Collecting special offerings, such as One Great Hour of Sharing, Native American Awareness Sunday, or Rural Life Sunday
4. Recycling and contributing the proceeds to an outreach project
5. Sponsoring a refugee family (easier when two or three churches do it together)
6. Organizing voter registration
7. Holding political office
8. Being involved in issues that effect your county, state, or region (such as farm crisis, and so on)

Organize and Assess Your Church's Outreach Ministries

Form a team of people who will work on developing outreach ministries. Begin by asking the following questions:

1. What outreach ministries does your church financially support?

2. How do your church members actively participate in (that is, "do") outreach ministries?

3. Inventory the outreach ministries taking place at your church. You may wish to categorize them as follows:

                        Support Financially   *"Hands-on" Ministries*
   a. Local community
   b. State
   c. National
   d. International

4. Share and discuss the information gathered during the community interviews.
- What needs exist in your community?
- What talents, abilities, and experiences exist among your members that could be used to address these needs?
- Think and talk about the needs of your state, nation, and world. What needs currently exist?
- How might your congregation address these needs?

It is important to develop a balance of ministries aimed at local, state, national, and international concerns. Also work to develop a balance between outreach ministries that your church supports financially and those in which church members actively participate.

Witness Ministries

The ministry of witness gives people the opportunity to share their faith understanding of personal and corporate salvation, reconciliation, worship, celebration, spiritual development, and discipline. It also provides people with opportunities to share their faith with other persons and to work for justice, righteousness, and the redemption of the world.

The Book of Discipline (¶251.2.c) defines the work of witness ministries as follows:

> The witness ministries . . . shall give attention to developing and strengthening evangelistic efforts of sharing of personal and congregational stories of Christian experience, faith, and service; communications; lay speaking ministries; and other means which give expressions of witness for Jesus Christ.

Biblical Basis: A careful reading of the New Testament tells us that the first Christians were drawn to the faith for a variety of reasons. This should not surprise us because we know that a witness approach that appeals to one person may not appeal to another. For example, the Acts of the Apostles depicts people being drawn to the early church for a variety of reasons. In Acts 2:14–42, on the day of Pentecost the disciples spoke to the people who came to Jerusalem in their native tongues. They gave testimony to God's deeds of power to thousands of people. Three thousand people responded to their testimony and were baptized on that very day.

Acts 17:16-32 describes a different reason people are drawn to the gospel. In this passage the apostle Paul is in Athens. He speaks to Epicurean and Stoic philosophers, taking an intellectual approach to describe the gift of salvation to them. Upon hearing of the Resurrection, some of the philosophers scoffed, some agreed to hear Paul again, and some became believers.

Acts 8:26–40 relates the account of Philip initiating a relationship with an Ethiopian eunuch a court official of Candace, queen of Ethiopia in order to share with him the story of the Christian faith. The Holy Spirit urged Philip to run to the eunuch's chariot and join him. There Philip learned that the eunuch was reading Scripture, but could not understand it. He invited Philip to ride in the chariot and explain the words to him. Philip did this, relating the passage being read from Isaiah to the good news of Jesus Christ. The result was that the eunuch stopped the chariot, and Philip baptized him. A recurrent theme found throughout Acts is that people respond to a personal invitation to hear and believe the story of Christ. Peter, Paul, and the other apostles again and again invite people to believe in salvation through Jesus Christ, and many respond in faith. The invitation to come, hear, believe, and belong is repeated throughout this book of the Bible.

Witness Ministries Today

Most people who become members of churches with small membership are attracted to the congregation because of one or more of the following reasons:

- They are born into the congregation;
- They are attracted to the ministry of the pastor, often because of the pastor's ministry to them during a personal crisis;
- They find a warm, intimate, family-type fellowship in the congregation;
- They are able to fill a need in the church's ministry;
- They are recruited through participation in a fellowship or service group related to the church, for example, the choir, scouts, and so forth.

Expanding Our View of Witness Ministries

The Great Commission of Jesus Christ is plain and simple: Christians are supposed to tell others about the gospel and encourage them to be baptized in the name of Jesus Christ. There are four building blocks for witness ministries in any church, including the small church:

- First, a concern for unchurched persons living in your community and a willingness to befriend these persons with Christian love
- Second, a commitment to talk to God about your concern for these persons
- Third, a willingness to develop effective and appropriate skills for sharing your faith with those who have no faith or who may have lost it along the way, which includes planning for witness ministries in your church
- Fourth, a pastor and lay leaders willing to teach members of your church how to accomplish the first three building blocks

People do not make a commitment to Jesus Christ by chance. They do not learn by accident what faith demands regarding their relationship with humanity, other living things, and the land with all its rich resources. Witness ministries must be thoughtfully planned and implemented.

Another concern to be addressed is whether people who visit your church can become accepted members of your congregation. Most churches with small membership like to think of themselves as "friendly, happy families." However, friendliness does not guarantee that new members will easily become part of your church family. Just like most families, your church family has a shared history, language, and behavior. Would you still feel the welcome and support of the congregation if *you* were the visitor? of a different ethnic background? an elderly person? a teenager with an earring?

Newcomers must be offered ways to learn (and longtime members need to be reminded of) this family background in order to be truly integrated into the congregation. They must also be offered a meaningful role in their new church family that includes sharing faith and ministry focus they believe they may be called toward. There are several ways to accomplish this:
- Tell the congregation's story on United Methodist Heritage Sunday.
- Assign new members and friends a mentor from the congregation. The role of the mentor is to make the newcomers feel acquainted, to facilitate their adoption into the congregation, and to help them discover opportunities for study, fellowship, and service in the church.
- Include newcomers in opportunities for fun and play. Congregations, like all families, need to play together in order to enjoy each other's company and to learn more about each other.

Build Upon Knowledge of Your Community

An accurate awareness of both the unchurched people in your community and the potential for numerical growth in your church is absolutely essential in planning for effective witness ministries. Before you begin reviewing or developing ministries of witness, however, invite church leaders and members to research data that impacts your community (make specific assignments). Data research should include the following:

1. The 2000 United States Census Bureau population (or other-up-to date) statistical data for your community. Call your district conference office for the demographics of your community. You may also obtain demographic information from the General Board of Global Ministries Web page.

2. The breakdown of the total population into the following age groups:
    - 0–5 years
    - 6–17 years
    - 18–29 years
    - 30–47 years
    - 48–65 years
    - 66–80 years
    - 81 + years

(Note: The local school superintendent's office, or even the school bus garage should have some figures on record. Other sources include your public library, or the Internet.)

3. Total number of churches and other houses of worship in your community:
    a. Number of members for each
    b. Average attendance for each

4. On the basis of the answers you receive to numbers 1 and 3 above, determine the number and the percentage of unchurched persons in your community.

5. Again, determine the following using the United States Census information:
    a. Percentage of racial or ethnic persons in your community
    b. Annual number of newcomers to the community

6. Identify and describe the kinds of persons in your community who, for whatever reason, are difficult to love.

7. Who are the impoverished, hardworking, unchurched persons in your community?

8. Who are the persons in your community who cannot worship on Sunday morning because of their work schedule or disability?

Examples of Witness Ministries

> These ideas are intended to generate the development of witness ministries in your church rather than to serve as a grab bag for activity.

Sometimes small churches have a "fuzziness" regarding the need for and the nature of witness ministries. It may be an avenue of ministry that your church is not intentional about doing. This is cause for concern. It should also be noted that there could be very close parallels between some witness ministries and some outreach ministries that are designed to address the structures and values of society and move toward justice and righteousness.

Speaking/Word Witness Ministries

1. Church members telling their friends, relatives, coworkers, fellow students, and others about the meaning of the Christian faith
2. A door-to-door community canvass, including the extension of an invitation to worship (informative doorhangers—like the ones pizza shops use—may be used)
3. Distribution of a brochure explaining church services and programs
4. Providing worship services at nursing homes
5. Sponsoring a lay speaking course in your church
6. Visiting people who visit church
7. Offering a concert with contemporary Christian music, open to the community
8. Outdoor tent revival services
9. A preschool program with Christian emphasis
10. A newsletter mailed to all persons in the community
11. Presenting a Last Supper, Nativity, or Easter drama, open to the entire community
12. Community youth groups that seek youth from the entire community
13. Organize a revival or church renewal day that offers contemporary ways to pray and experience God, planned by people from the church and community
14. Christian recreation program for children during the summer
15. Settings for recovering addicts who want to live the Christian life
16. Family, youth, or children rallies
17. Add a section to your prayer list, "People who do not know Christ," and pray for these people (even if you do not know their name!)
18. Train people to give a testimony of what God is doing in their life and provide settings for this type of sharing

Doing/Action Witness Ministries
1. Make the church sanctuary available to the community for funerals, memorial services, and weddings; but have clear policies approved by the trustees
2. Share in ecumenical worship services
3. Public service that builds up the community and addresses human needs
4. Church building construction such as a Christian life center, or renovation that shows that the church is alive and active
5. Peaceful protests and demonstrations in the community to bring about awareness of social ills and to press for actions to resolve those problems
6. Church-sponsored scholarship program for graduating seniors
7. Recycling
8. Mobilization of community resistance to hard liquor sales, drug sales and usage, and so forth
9. The individual Christian lifestyles of church members
10. A church-sponsored county fair booth, offering free, cold water and a place to sit in the shade
11. Build or refurbish a playground for children
12. Go to places in your community where tragedy may have occurred and provide a service of worship in that place
13. Encourage church members to host a backyard VBS in their homes for children around them who are not a part of the church

Good Communication Enhances Witness

Effective smaller congregations use good public relations techniques. Some churches may feel uneasy about thinking of public relations as a way to witness to their faith. However, it is an indispensable part of witnessing to the local community.

There are three important keys to doing effective public relations. They are: advertise, advertise, and advertise. That is, keep the story of your church's ministries in front of the public as much as possible. This can be achieved in several ways:
- Place temporary signs in front of the church. These signs should be attractively designed and used to promote such activities as vacation Bible school, special seasonal programs, rally days, and so forth.
- As a general rule, make some recognizable change to the outside of your church building and property annually. This reminds the community that your church is active and present within the community and gives it a fresh look. The change need not be substantial. Something as simple as putting an attractive canvas banner across the front of the building, planting different colored annual flowers, or painting the front door a different color is enough to attract the attention of those who pass by.

- Make good use of your local newspaper. While it is helpful to include your church in the listing of worship services, articles describing the ministries of your congregation and upcoming events are more effective.
- When decorating the church for celebrations, do not forget the outside of the building. Wreaths and lights are helpful during Advent and Christmas. A simple wooden cross draped with purple fabric during Lent and changed to white during Eastertide is especially attractive.

Being Intentional Is the Key

You may find you need more preparation for doing witness ministries than for nurture and outreach ministries. Perhaps your pastor has little or no training or experience in this type of ministry. If that is the case, then the pastor may need to attend a continuing education event designed to give direction, resources, and ideas for how you can do witness ministries together.

Members of the congregation may need to participate in a witness ministry training event or series of workshops. While this type of training should be made available to anyone who wishes to participate, it may be helpful for the pastor, lay leader or witness committee chairperson to pick several key persons to be trained.

If your congregation feels that there is potential for numerical growth in your community, you may want to consider forming a "church growth team." Such a team would consist of the following persons:
- Pastor
- Statistician
- New member development worker (who assists new members in becoming involved in the congregation)
- Church council chairperson
- Youth sponsor
- Sunday School superintendent
- Outreach captain (who focuses the congregation's attention on reaching out to unchurched persons)

The church growth team's primary responsibility is to devise, resource, and monitor church growth ministries in the congregation. Members of the team should not be seen as the only ones responsible for this work, but as coordinators and coparticipants in this ministry.

1. Based on the local data you have collected, is it possible that effective witness ministries might result in numerical growth for your congregation? Why or why not?

2. How do people become a part of your congregation? Do they reflect the biblical situations described in this resource?

3. Do people who have become part of your church in recent years reflect ways that people become members of small churches as described in this resource?

4. How does your church understand witness ministries?

5. Do you personally know unchurched people? Are there unchurched people in your community? Is your congregation equipped to do effective witness ministries?

6. What witness ministries are currently taking place at your church?

7. What witness ministries would you like your congregation to add to those being accomplished already?

Resource Ministries (rm)

Resource ministries—including the work of the *church council, committee on finance, pastor-parish relations committee,* and *board of trustees*—provide an essential supportive role in mobilizing the work of the small church. These resource ministries effectively utilize human resources, economic support, facilities, organizational and administrative processes, and linkages with the United Methodist connection and the church universal. Consult *The Book of Discipline* (¶258.4) for further description of the committee on finance, board of trustees, pastor-parish relations committee, and church treasurer.

Remember that the work of organizing and administering the church's ministries always requires careful planning, implementation, and evaluation. While the work of administration and organization of the church's ministries is absolutely essential, it is never an end in itself; it must always be seen as a means to bring about the actual program ministries of the church.

Trustees

The trustees manage the building and site as a resource for ministry. They ensure that everything is in proper working order. One of their tasks is to review the site as a place for ministry and make sure that everything is easily located and accessible. For definitions and responsibilities of the trustees, see *The Book of Discipline* (¶258.3; ¶¶2524–2549).

Imagine that you are a visitor to the church with little or no knowledge of the floor plan. Take a brief tour of the interior and exterior of the building from that person's perspective:

1. *How easy is it to locate key places,* such as the sanctuary, office, fellowship areas, learning spaces, and restrooms? Do you rely on the directions of others, or is it like playing "hide and seek"? When you walk in the door, how do you identify where to go for different spaces or purposes? If you were in a wheelchair, how easy would it be to maneuver the hallways and levels in the building?
2. *Is the appearance appealing and pleasant?* What do you see, smell, feel, and touch? Are surfaces clean, well lit? Does the color and texture of the walls seem bright and open or dark and depressing?
3. *Does each room or space look well cared for and clean,* or cluttered and dusty? Plan a workday to spruce up the church.
4. *Make a note of any necessary improvements and develop a plan for renovation with other trustees.*
5. *Is the building a safe place for people to be?*

Beyond facility appearance and function, managing risk reduction and guaranteeing safety both in the facility and during church activities (on- and off-site) is important!

Trustees are responsible for providing a place for ministry for groups in the church, as well as those from the community (such as scouts). Do you have a policy for using and securing the building that allows it to be utilized? Are things labeled for where they go in the church and how a visitor to the facility can find things and return them to their proper place?

Finance

The responsibilties of the finance committee can be found in *The Discipline,* (¶258.4.)

Developing a budget can both interpret and support ministry. Using the NOW(rm) model as a guide for developing the church's general budget is another way to interpret the model—and the focus on ministry—to the congregation. A church budget set up in this fashion is not only an informative interpretation tool, it is also a theological document that clearly delineates the Christian ministries of the congregation. Consider using the NOW(rm) model for outlining your line item budget.

Raising money for ministry is essential. There are many ways to raise money for ministry in the small membership church:

Offerings	Special appeals
Fund-raisers	Capital improvement gifts
Memorials	Sales
Rent for space	Financial partnerships with others
Grants	Conference funds
Booktables	Foundations

> A key to financially supporting ministry is intentionally setting guidelines for fund-raising. Another consideration is finding out where the grant sources are in your area.

Developing ministry partnerships with others can be good stewardship. The small membership church knows how to work together. How well does your congregation work with other churches or groups? Examples of partnerships that work are those you make locally, such as youth ministry shared with another congregation, children's preschool organized by the YWCA, and so on. Realize you do not have to do it all yourself!

Pastor-Parish

The pastor (staff) parish relations committee, or team, is defined in *The Discipline,* (¶258.2). The main focus of this group is to help bridge the gifts and abilities of the pastor and laity in the church.

Building bridges that link the faithfulness of the past with the possibilities of the future is crucial. Pastor-parish committees that want to do effective work will learn about the following:
- Understanding the nature of chaos and change
- Resolving conflict
- Establishing a covenant to guide behavior
- Developing clear, open communication
- Developing ministry support from district strategies (especially inside the church) conferences and general church agencies

Committee on Lay Leadership

The work of this committee is found in *The Discipline,* (¶258.1). Think of this group in your church as the gardeners, whose task is to nourish the roots of the plants. In a church, it is this team that identifies the gifts of individuals and provides training and support for ministry.

An engaged lay leadership committee will offer opportunities for spiritual growth that include spiritual gift discovery. The committee (or team) members will also take the time to talk with people in leadership positions to find out their experience of serving in the church. Pay particular attention to what the leadership believes they have accomplished, what would have helped support their work in the last year, and what improvements can be made in leading.

> The finance, pastor-parish, nominations and personnel committees, and the trustees should occasionally meet together to coordinate their support of ministry and communicate with one another.

Eight NOW(rm) Keys for Transforming Current Ministry

Believe it: church leaders are looking for a better way to be in ministry—ways that are effective. These need not produce more meetings, but they should produce meaningful ministries. Review the following keys and transform your church leadership into a team that works together for vital ministry.

Key 1: Small Steps Lead to Greater Strides

Taking the right small steps can lead to a greater awareness of ministry potential in your church. Begin by talking to one or more key leaders about using this model to mobilize ministry. Ask how they could work together to be successful in implementing this organization. Listen to their concerns, as well as their supportive comments. Invite these individuals to help explain this model to others in the church council or main leadership group.

Set a trial period to explore the potential of using NOW(rm) in your church (for example, six months). Let people know that at the end of this period everyone will have the opportunity to evaluate its success and make adjustments. Ask everyone to pray for the ministry of the church and for each other during this time. Establish prayer partners.

Key 2: Carefully Communicate This Design for Ministry

This needs to be done in more than one way, in more than one setting: (for example, letters to leadership or members, visits with individuals and groups, announcements in worship, invitations to pray for discernment, leadership training settings) Let church leaders choose which ministry area their position fits in the best. Choice is important! People feel better able to turn problems into possibilities if they also have the freedom to make choices! Invite everyone to commit to the success of this organization.

One of the biggest challenges involved in mobilizing the small church for effective ministry is moving beyond ministries that "feel comfortable and good" to ministries that challenge the church's membership. This is truly a step that requires spiritual courage and Christian bravery!

As you review the work your small church is doing in each of these areas, develop a plan that retains those ministries you deem to be most appropriate, while adding those nurture, outreach, and witness ministries you deem to be most needed. Check your resource ministries and be sure they are designed to help you do what God is calling you to do in the areas of nurture, outreach, and witness. Put all of this on paper. Circulate it to members of the church council for suggestions and changes. When you finish, you will have your "NOW(rm) Action Plan."

Key 3: Examine Your Current Ministry Within the Last Two Years

List each and every activity, program, event, study, service project, and small group, offered by the church under the appropriate heading—nurture, outreach, witness, or resource ministries. Take a moment and compare the lists. What do you notice? Is ministry balanced or lopsided?

Key 4: Decide Wherever Possible—One Ministry Focus

Leaders in the small church are often generalists (including the pastor!). It is not uncommon for the same person to be the Sunday School superintendent, president of the United Methodist Women, teach a children's Sunday School class, and play organ in worship. If these leadership positions fall under one category, no problem. (This is just a very involved nurture team member!) Be aware of people who hold key positions in more than one ministry focus, such as nurture and outreach. It is difficult to serve on two different ministry teams and still be an active, supportive participants in both.

One of the key lessons from NOW(rm) is the nature of teams. A team is a group of individuals with different talents and gifts committed to working together on a specific focus. Always look for opportunities to develop teams by inviting new people to serve on ministry planning groups, especially for a specific event or a project with a specific time span.

Key 5: Plan with the End in Mind, Not at Your Wit's End

Ministry fails when insufficient attention is given to the details:
- Who is being served;
- What will be done;
- Why it is important;
- How it will be done;
- When and where it will happen;
- By whom and and how we will know we have been successful.

When we simply take an idea and replicate it without regard to these details being fully considered, we drain the limited resources of the church and unintentionally build a climate for failure. *Plan!* Some churches plan for ministry throughout the year in teams or committees, while others have quarterly sessions or an annual leadership planning retreat. *When* you plan is not as important as *how well* you plan!

Key 6: Use an Agenda

The agenda for the meeting states clearly the focus for coming together. The agenda helps the flow of the meeting so that people leave with a sense of accomplishment and purpose. An agenda sets the priorities and establishes relationships among leaders.

Consider a New Agenda. One of the most dangerous ailments of ineffective churches is that of doing the same things repeatedly, even when results are poor or unsatisfactory. This is often observed in the way church leaders set their agendas and conduct church meetings. Several years ago *Net Results,* a publication featuring new ideas in church vitality and leadership, suggested that church council/board meetings could be better structured by emphasizing the spiritual life of the congregation and celebrating its ministries. Based on the NOW(rm) model, an agenda for this kind of church council meeting might look like this:

Opening (5 minutes) Tell about an outreach/mission program in the church that is working. Opening prayer.

Celebration of the Church Alive (10–15 minutes)
- Report on the average attendance at Sunday school and worship, noting the number of visitors
- Report on the membership total and constituency list totals
- Brief observance of any deaths, including a celebration of older "saints" who have joined the church triumphant, or an expression of shared grief over the loss of a younger person
- Brief celebration of new baptisms and church memberships

- Setting of attendance goals for the next month
- Brief informal report on how the church is bringing about spiritual growth in the congregation
- Provide an update on any ministry that is being shared with another congregation or group.
- Pray that members will remain faithful, that newcomers will be invited, and that both groups will be in church often this month; the pastor may also wish to share concerns and prayer requests

Reports from Program Groups or Teams (20 minutes)
- Nurture ministry group
- Outreach ministry group
- Witness ministry group
- President, United Methodist Men
- President, United Methodist Women
- President, United Methodist Youth Council
- Superintendent, church school
- Lay leader
- Other programmatic reports, as necessary

Again, the primary emphasis should be on what is bringing excitement and joy to the congregation. This is also the time for the work areas to recommend new programs for Church Council approval.

Minutes of the Last Meeting and Resource Ministry Reports (15 minutes total)
- Reports (financial secretary, church treasurer, committee on finance)
- Committee on pastor-parish relations
- Committee on lay leadership
- Board of trustees

This is the time to address how these groups can continue to undergird and support what is happening. Is the number of paid staff adequate? Is the building large enough and in good repair for these kinds of activities? Are the financial receipts sufficient to cover what God is bringing about in this church? Has the church council done what it said it would do? Are the church's programmatic goals being met?

If the answers to these questions are yes, then celebrate! If the answers are no, then decide what the congregation and staff need to do in order to create more effective ministries.

> *The Book of Discipline* affirms the use of this agenda model in ¶251.3.b:

> In order that the council may give adequate consideration to the missional purpose of the local church, it is recommended that the first agenda item at each of its meetings shall be related to its ministries of nurture, outreach, and witness. The administrative and supportive responsibilities of the church will then be given attention. It is also recommended that the council use a consensus/discernment decision-making style.

The church council needs to practice careful agenda planning and spiritual discernment. One small church requires that all "action items" coming from committees and ministry groups be available in printed form for distribution to church council members on the Sunday prior to their regular meeting. This allows time for thoughtful consideration and asking questions about the item. It also provides time for *spiritual discernment,* or knowing what is best for the congregation and its ministries (Philippians 1:9–10.) Developing this spiritual ability to distinguish good from evil is of utmost importance when planning the ministries of your church (Hebrews 5:12–14). The primary operational question here is "What does God think?" Careful attention to this question necessitates providing the time and format needed.

Most small churches find that in addressing action items *consensus agreements work far better than majority votes.* Consensus is a "win-win" process. An action item is discussed until everyone in the group is either in agreement with its approval or disapproval. Sometimes referring the item back to the ministry group or committee from which it came for further shaping is appropriate. On the other hand, majority/minority voting is a "win-lose" process. The majority wins, while the minority loses. This can cause dissension and hard feelings. Consensus agreements take more work, but in the long run they are the healthiest decision-making process.

Key 7: Celebrate! Keep Your Eye on the Energy Level of People Involved in Ministry

The point of using the NOW(rm) model is not "busy-ness" (or business), but depth (helping people grow in faith). Celebrate what is being done and what is being learning as you plan and implement ministry together. Recognize and encourage others for their hard work. Offer training and resources so that others can be effective.

Key 8: Develop and Use a Calendar

A planning calendar, whether it is maintained by the pastor or key lay leader, is essential in smaller congregations. Ministry groups and other committees should check with this calendar before scheduling church programs and events. It is also appropriate for the church council to supervise this calendar.

If you use these eight keys, you can work together in your church and turn potential problems into opportunities for ministry and growth! The ministry of your church can be a blessing *NOW!* Leaders in the church, members of the congregation, and people in the community will benefit from your hard work and dedication to discipleship.

You are at the end of this booklet, *but you are at the beginning of the next moment of ministry.* It is our hope that you join with others in your congregation and community to offer an effective ministry. Build on your strengths and develop ministries that nurture, reach out to those in need, and witness to the grace and love of Jesus Christ. Be about the vital task of making disciples. *Make a difference!*

Resources

Small Membership Church Leadership and Ministry

Thomas G. Bandy. *Growing Spiritual Redwoods* (Abingdon Press, 1996).

Thomas G. Bandy. *Moving Off the Map* (Abingdon Press, 1998).

Steve Bierly. *Help for the Small Church Pastor: Unlocking the Potential of Your Congregation* (Zondervan Publishing, 1995).

Steve Bierely. *How to Thrive as a Small Church Pastor: A Guide to Spiritual and Emotional Well Being* (Zondervan Publishing, 1998).

Ronald K. Crandall. *Turnaround Strategies for the Small Church* (Nashville: Abingdon Press, 1995).

Deborah K. Cronin. *O for a Dozen Tongues to Sing* (Abingdon Press, 1996).

Dan R. Dick and Evelyn Burry. *Quest: A Journey Toward a New Kind of Church* (Discipleship Resources, 1999).

Shannon L. Jung and Mary A. Agria. *Rural Ministry, The Shape of The Renewal to Come* (Abingdon Press, 1998).

Ronald Klassen and John Koessler. *No Little Places: The Untapped Potential of the Small Church* (Baker Books, 1996).

Alice Mann, *Can Our Church Live?* (The Alban Institute, 2000).

Alice Mann, *The In-Between Church* (The Alban Institute, 1999)

Julia Wallace, *Small Churches Can Make a Big Difference* (Video; Discipleship Resources, 1999).

General Board of Discipleship Staff: Julia Wallace, Small Membership Church and Shared Ministries; Herb Mather, Stewardship; Dean McIntyre, Music. Write to them at: General Board of Discipleship, P.O. Box 340003, Nashville, TN 37203-0003.

Nurture Ministries

Discipleship Resources Comprehensive Catalog, P.O. Box 340003, Nashville, TN 37203-0003 (800-685-4370). Catalog features books and other resources designed to produce growth in Christian faith and life.

Upper Room Publications, P.O. Box 189, Nashville, TN 37202). The Upper Room publishes a variety of resources designed to nurture Christians, including *The Upper Room Magazine* (a daily devotional guide), *Pockets* (for children ages 6-12), and *Alive Now!* (a devotional magazine with a topical approach). *Weavings: A Journal of the Christian Spiritual Life* explores the many ways in which God's life and human lives are woven together. The Upper Room also provides numerous programs designed to assist Christians in spiritual formation, such as the Walk to Emmaus.

Bibles. Strange as it may seem, few churches offer a supply of Bibles to their members, other than for use in the Sunday school or sanctuary. The American Bible Society sells a variety of Bibles, many of which are available at low cost for distribution. Cokesbury, the United Methodist bookstore, also sells a variety of Bibles and Bible study aids.

DISCIPLE: Becoming Disciples Through Bible Study is an excellent 34-week study program designed to help persons become and grow as disciples through Bible study (offered through Cokesbury).

Outreach Ministries

The General Board of Global Ministries Service Center Catalog is a primary resource for learning about outreach ministries. It includes resources for pastors, missions or outreach local church lay leadership, United

Methodist Women, committees on health and welfare ministries, and church school leaders. Available through the Service Center, 7820 Reading Road, Caller No. 1800, Cincinnati, Ohio 45222-1800.

Prayer Calendar, available through the Service Center. Provides daily guidance in prayer for work and workers of the General Board of Global Ministries.

Partnership in Mission, available through the Service Center. Lists and describes all world, national, and United Methodist Committee on Relief General Advance Projects.

New World Outlook, available through the Service Center. The mission magazine of United Methodism. Includes current information about United Methodist missions, mission education in the local church, material for youth and children, Bible studies, photo essays, and more.

Witness Ministries

Joseph C. Aldrich, *Gentle Persuasion* (Multnomah Books, 1988). Teaches pastors and congregations how to approach unchurched persons with winsome, irresistible witnessing.

John M. Freeman, *Biblical Virtues,* Vital Ministry in the Small Membership Church Series (General Board of Discipleship, 1999). Teaches leaders of the small church how to focus on its unique virtues.

H. Eddie Fox and George E. Morris, *Faith-Sharing* (Discipleship Resources, 1996). Trains people to develop a personalized approach to evangelism that is direct and inviting to others.

Betty Whitehurst, *Mission,* Vital Ministry in the Small Membership Church Series (General Board of Discipleship, 1999). Offers concrete suggestions for small congregations to reach beyond themselves.

Resource Ministries

Church Council, Guidelines for Leading Your Congregation 2001–2004. Provides guidance for persons responsible for the administration and program of the local church.

Deborah K. Cronin, *Superintending the Small Church in the 21st Century,* Vital Ministry in the Small Membership Church Series (General Board of Discipleship, 1999). Leads the District Superintendent to be a partner in the success of small churches.

FaithQuest: A Vision for Leadership in the Local Church. A resource for congregational leaders to engage in a process of learning, visioning, planning, and transformation, centered in Scripture. Contact the FaithQuest Office at the General Board of Discipleship.

Net Results, 12 issues per year. 5001 Avenue North, Lubbock, TX 79412-2993. Provides creative ideas for church growth, programming, and leadership.

A Resource Notebook for Cooperative Parish Ministries (available from Cooperative Ministry Resources, P.O. Box 267, Sylvania, AL 35988). An excellent new tool that describes how cooperative ministries can vitalize congregations and transform communities.

Small Churches Can Make a Big Difference: A Resource for Small Membership Church Leaders. A 29-minute video that showcases three small congregations that are transforming lives. Available from Discipleship Resources. An 8-page leader's guide is included.